MIDCENTURY MODERN: 15 INTERIOR DESIGN IDEAS

AS SEEN IN THE QUEEN'S GAMBIT

I. NGEOW

Written and illustrated by I. Ngeow

This book has been written in US English.

First published in Great Britain in 2021 by Leopard Print

Copyright © 2021 by I. Ngeow

All rights reserved.

CONTENTS

INTRODUCTION

The initial ideas that sparked this book came from my architectural and design profession, TV (the Queen's Gambit, Mad Men and Twin Peaks), travel (Miami and Vegas opened my eyes), Hitchcock movies and modern American literature.

HOW TO INTERIOR DESIGN LIKE THE QUEEN'S GAMBIT

This handbook is a style guide aimed at amateurs, designers or enthusiasts. By bringing together popular culture of TV and the spaces which surround us, I have come up with 15 ideas for inspiration to start us off on a midcentury modern journey to creating looks from the Queen's Gambit. You can use them in a combo, separately or as a springboard to your own style portfolio. Each chapter has a **HOT TIP** to further amp up any design and give it the professional touch.

The Queen's Gambit has been described as a maximalist style with minimalist design. It is not for those who baulk at "stuff" or dislike color. There are no neutrals except the chessboard. Kondo your fear and combo your thoughts! The beauty of midcentury modern design is balance. With the right lighting, color, finishes and simple interesting furniture, you will have a perfectly workable "form follows function" modern space configuration that works.

This book does not cover modern graphic design which was largely instigated by the Bauhaus movement. Minimalist, blocky modern sans serif typography that we use now had its roots in the midcentury era. Flat, minimal colors and abstract shapes filled modern art, book covers, travel advertisements and movie posters such as those of Saul Bass for Hitchcock movies.

Although the scope of this book will also not include literary criticism, the works of Patricia Highsmith, Ernest Hemingway, John Steinbeck and Harper Lee have always been my big influences when I was growing up.

WHAT IS MIDCENTURY MODERN?

Midcentury modern has been used to describe a design aesthetic, in particular, furniture, but it actually refers to the golden age of architecture and design. Midcentury modern, which began its ascent in the 1930s after Art Deco and Art Moderne, lasted into the 1970s. Purists might like to insist that it is a precise post-World War II decade from 1947 to 1957.

The principles of midcentury modern design are still practiced today. Elegance and simplicity have evolved from origins of the modernist mantra:

"Form follows function"- Louis Sullivan[1]

The phrase originated from Louis H. Sullivan in his 1896 essay, "The Tall Office Building Artistically Considered." Often called America's first modern architect, Louis Sullivan (1856-1924) was born in Boston, Massachusetts. Pioneer of the Midwest American skyscraper, he influenced architectural language which became known as the Chicago School. Mentor to his young apprentice, Frank Lloyd Wright (1867-1959), Sullivan's design philosophy was the "multi-use building", which is still discussed and practiced today. As he professionally matured, Wright challenged the original dogma of "form follows function", concluding that, in fact, "form and function are one"[2].

Midcentury modern is about understated ornamentation and problem-solving. All mass-produced housing, buildings and modern furniture are based on midcentury design principles.

Though it is now roughly 60-80 years old, it's a never-gone-out-of-style style. This is because it's not really a style but more a design philosophy, an eclectic movement, which overlaps with other styles of the time. Traditionally, it has been viewed as an American movement, which in turn has developed from European, South American and other global modernist languages. The International Style or the Bauhaus movement is a strong influence, for example. The postwar aesthetic was an important factor in the design of houses and the modernization of American suburbs.

"Midcentury modernism is a living concept. It will be applicable forever."- William Krisel[3]

ARCHITECTURE

Midcentury modern architecture is the most well-defined category of the movement. The endeavor and focus of post-war architecture has always been to reimagine modern life and to ease the horrors of World War II. Ideas were spreading quickly on how to solve problems in a minimal and more efficient way and how to create new and exciting spatial configurations. Regular suburban people had the opportunity and access to modern good design.

This ethos for living spaces is alive even today. All if not many of the ideas of transparency, openness and a connection to nature are considered the pillars of good architecture. Large horizontal opening windows, ample daylight entering and flooding a space, flat roofs, open plan living leading to the outdoor space, use of natural materials like stone and wood... these are solid principles that will never date. Midcentury modernism did not just stay in the postwar American residential suburb. It extended to public buildings, infrastructure and municipal architecture.

FURNITURE

Furniture and industrial design followed architectural principles. "Multipurpose became a catchphrase," wrote Cara Greenberg in *Midcentury Modern: Furniture of the 1950s* explaining that "this new furniture stacked, folded and bent; it was rearrangeable and inter-changeable; it nested and flexed. Chairs were designed to be pressed into service for a dozen different reasons. Tables were non-specific, for eating, writing, or playing cards."[4]

It was very forward thinking for 60 years ago. That same furniture has its purpose today, which is multipurpose. Minimalist furniture, lacking in ornamentation was so popular that even the structural elements were minimized to make the furniture appear lighter, such as the thin legs, and hairpin legs.

Simplicity is a key concept of midcentury modern design. Chairs were simplified, from seat to back in one continuous shape, for example, the Eames shell chair. Wooden Scandinavian furniture, in clean streamlined curved shapes, is still highly-sought after. The radical shapes come from experimenting and challenging traditional ideas, for example, the Egg chair by Arne Jacobson which has a bold shape and is one-legged rather than four.

I hope I have whet your appetite and that you will get to the end, where there are three BONUS midcentury classic cocktail recipes awaiting you. If you're ready, let's start with our first design idea.

1. Sullivan, Louis H. "The Tall Office Building Artistically Considered." Lippincott's Magazine, March 1896.

2. Wright, Frank Lloyd. "The Future of Architecture." New American Library, Horizon Press, 1953.

3. Krisel, William. "Palm Springs: The Language of Modernism", Gibbs Smith, 2016

4. Greenberg, Cara, *Midcentury Modern: Furniture of the 1950s*, Three Rivers Press (1995)

ONE

WINGED ARMCHAIRS

THE WINGED ARMCHAIR is a restful piece of furniture in which we have seen Alma Wheatley (Beth Harmon's adoptive mother) relaxing or having a drink next to the grand piano. It is in the teal velvet winged armchair that she has a few conversations with Beth.

The winged armchair is a high-backed armchair providing support and even some privacy should you wish to doze. I have one myself with buttons and it's from the I-word (the Swedish flatpack furniture conglomerate who also manufacture meatballs). They have quite a few reproductions that are well-designed, value for money, surprisingly sturdy and unsurprisingly non flatpack.

Fabrics are tough and durable. Recommended fabrics include linen, boucle and of course, velvet. **HOT TIP:** Add a matching foot-stool and we're in heaven.

Cushions, if any, should be in a contrasting fabric and color, for example, wool, felt or silk.

TWO
BOTANICAL

Pink and green is a fresh and striking color palette for a botanical
theme in the European whimsical style.

WALLPAPER MADE a big appearance in the Queen's Gambit. In one
scene, Beth's entire bedroom had matching floral chintz wallpaper
and bedding. Not an inch was left uncovered. Nowadays, that would
be over-the-top but not unacceptable. It is more popular and trendy

to have a feature wall, papered with an exciting and vibrant tropical or botanical design theme.

HOT TIP: Bold wallpaper has to be in scale and promotion to the size of the wall to visually create a mood or an impact. The larger the wall, the larger the pattern should be.

This bedroom is reminiscent of the pink, white and red floral chintz in Beth Harmon's room.

Midcentury modern furniture in this contemporary design with a botanical-themed wallpaper brings this room up to date. This living space doubles as a perfect meeting breakout space or coffee area on a hotel mezzanine for example.

THREE

STRING CHAIRS

I REMEMBER GROWING up with these: the tropical concept of the light outdoor chair which you can sit in when you're wet to "drip-dry" yourself due to its spidery minimalist design. It is ideal for the indoor-outdoor space concept. My aunt still has a reclining sun lounger in the same steel frame and nylon string construction. They come in white or multi-colored. This was in the night time swimming scene from Beth Harmon's tournament in Mexico. As a poolside or patio decoration, the sunburst effect of the stringing is an attractive feature, bringing back nostalgic childhood moments for me.

HOT TIP: Bring this outdoor look up to date for that vintage industrial appeal, with little metal pedestal tables for resting drinks, a bowl of Doritos and the blockbuster you're reading.

FOUR

LITTLE TABLES

LITTLE COFFEE TABLES, often nested, are still quite popular now, thanks to the I-word. The Swedish flatpack furniture chain has produced these leaf shaped plywood tables shown, and rather practically, the smaller one can tuck back into the bigger table when not in use.

I am a fan of gold and glass. A little side table is so pretty and smart for resting coffee, cocktails or flowers. It is very delicate with its thin gold legs but you are able to move it from room to room. And of course, as my clients have told me, they are the perfect size for ugly plastic remote controls! You will never lose them again if you just look for the gold legs in the room.

There is also a timeless appeal of the little side table for lamps and providing a foreground to a wall. The table is usually not a feature, rather a backup or overspill area to the room's design or a feature wall. Balance is key to the placement of the little side table (the LST). **HOT TIP:** Group things to display. For example, all remotes together, all keys on a tray. Loose items like change, earrings etc should be collated on little ceramic trays or gold dishes to keep them together and make it easier for tidying and cleaning.

FIVE
PINK

ATOMIC DESIGN, Scandinavian cool and exotic or travel locations during the 1950s and 1960s influenced the rising popularity of pinks and greens in design due to the new post-World War II optimism and a hopeful future. Elvis Presley's favorite shirt color was apparently pink.

A spacious pastel pink bathroom paired with chartreuse chintz, like the one Beth is seen looking for her pills, highlights the suburban idyll. Chartreuse is a bright yellowish green which derives its name from the French liqueur. It is directly opposite pink on the color wheel therefore is complementary.

Black and gold are the perfect neutral companions to pink and green for a harmonious color combination. "Housewife" pink is often seen in Hawaiian or tropical print chintz, matched with black and white mosaics and gold accessories.

HOT TIP: Analogous to green on the color wheel is teal, and opposite green is pink. When all three are used adjacent to each other, they create that powerful vintage cinematic impact.

SIX

FURNITURE WITH THIN LEGS

FURNITURE WITH HAIRPIN or slim tapered legs is an important characteristic of the elegant modernist era. There was an emphasis on making furniture appear "floating" or lighter in mass than it is. Used in combination with glass, it's within the design principles of being light and transparent, thereby making the room appear bigger, especially as it contrasts with a strong teal or jewel-colored interior.

Commonly used is a nest of tables idea, where the little one fits
back into the bigger table, or slightly protrudes. The thin legs give the

illusion of a bigger space and smaller tables. Each table has brass cone-tipped stiletto legs.

On the pink velvet suite, the thin gold legs are also a feature of midcentury modern furniture, which is the touch of luxury to otherwise quite plain simple shapes. This compact 3-piece suite of furniture fits into a corner of a room. It is offset by a tall plant which once again makes the room look bigger when it is narrow and pinched in its proportion. The banana palm also blanks off what is in effect a dead space as the area is too small to put any other furniture. This is another common trick to offset leftover space, as modern architecture has a lot of interior angular corners in order to make the exterior streamlined.

HOT TIP: A small stool with thin legs is portable and multipurpose. It can be a coffee table, footrest, additional seating or even a stepladder, and therefore it is ideal for a small apartment or house.

SEVEN

CURTAINS

NIGHTS IN SATIN. Curtains are rich, luxurious and full length. Floor to ceiling curtains that we commonly only see in hotel rooms are for the purpose of blacking out the room. The neatness that comes with no visible rail, pole or track completes the window wall's minimal appearance. The curtains simply melt into the wall.

HOT TIP: Fabric should have a sheen or luster to provide good shadowing in its folds from table lamps and ceiling lighting. It can be used with a sheer curtain on a separate tracking. The curtains when shut should make the room appear like the window wall is indeed another wall, like a stage.

Take a look at a hotel room the next time you are in one. Stand in the window area and look up into the window reveal to check the tracking and the distance between the tracks. You will see that there are at least 2 tracks. The first track, innermost in the room, is the fabric you want to look at with a blackout lining sewn onto it, the second is the sheer fabric for day use.

Recommended fabrics are taffeta, Shantung dupion, crepe, polyester satin, silk jacquard or any silk mix. They should be light or medium weight to contrast with the heavy fabrics of the furniture. A very matte or patterned fabric like cotton or damask would not create glam or gleam in night lighting, and therefore is unsuitable for creating what I would call the Twin Peaks effect. Can you not see Agent Cooper standing in his suit in this room?

EIGHT

GOLD

PRETTY COFFEE CUPS and gold details are part of the maximalist
little luxuries. We see Beth mourning her mother when she comes
home from Mexico and notices the lipstick on the coffee cup that her

mother had been using. We also see gold in other fine details, like the watch she was given, and the little cocktail tables. The art to using gold in accessorizing and decorating is using only a tiny amount. **HOT TIP:** Small accents such as this gold tray and mini vase add a neat touch to otherwise deep-colored interiors.

NINE

SIDEBOARDS

IN THE DAYS before they became built-in like kitchen cabinets, sideboards were practical pieces of furniture for storage. Traditionally used in the dining room or for serving food, they can be for storing large serving dishes, and they can be a surface on which to place the record player. It is quite a social piece of furniture as it becomes part of the room when entertaining. It also can be used for displaying your sparse but interesting collection of *objets* and exotic plants.

The scale and height of the sideboard is important in a room layout as it is usually quite large and wooden yet has to be low enough to act as a counter top such that firstly, tall items such as a big bouquet of flowers or an impressive plant can still be at eye level. Secondly, a telephone, a record player, a little tray of keys can be easily utilized and accessed.

HOT TIP: To offset the bulky appearance and nature of the sideboard, midcentury modern sideboards have the characteristic high, thin or tapered legs. Opt for a large space under the sideboard rather than a tight space which is harder to clean. Aim to visually lift the room and make the floor area appear larger.

TEN

INDOOR PLANTS

Tropical indoor plants are very characteristic of the midcentury modern movement of using plants as sculpture and color.

Grown into window boxes, the large leafy nature of tropical plants provides internal screening. And a view if you have no view or an unpleasant view.

The purpose of the indoor plant is not to provide color (well, yes, just one color — green) but contrast and architectural value. The plants which were favored tended to be large-leaved and dark, with broad blades.

Top 5 recommendations for easy care indoor plants:

- Monstera deliciosa (Swiss cheese plant) is valued for its large form (finger-like palm leaves) and distinctive holes which cast good shadowing and make a stunning statement in any room.
- Epipremnum aureus (Devil's Ivy) is a fast-growing vine with heart-shaped mottled leaves. It is very pretty and can be suspended or placed at a higher level in a pot or basket due to the cascading vine leaves.
- Sanseviera (Mother-in-law's tongue). AKA the snake plant due to its reptilian looking leaves. This South African native has pointed succulent upright leaves.
- Anthurium Andreanum (Anthurium) is Colombian in origin and has dark green glossy leaves and deep red, pink or white heart-shaped flowers. The flowers are spathes (a leaf-like bract) which surround a cylindrical spike.
- Ficus elastics (Rubber Plant or Fig) has shiny rounded leaves in dark green and burgundy.

A quick research will bring up quite a few more but these five are low maintenance in my experience. **HOT TIP:** arrange plants in threes. Large sculptural shaped plants like the monstera and sansevieria work well when surrounded by two little plants like the ferns, vines or anthuriums.

ELEVEN
MEXICO

Taking its inspiration from Mexican art, this tri-colored tiled wall is striking and provides a feature wall in a bathroom. It can also be used as flooring.

HOT TIP: In any graphic or geometric pattern, the key to maximizing visual impact is firstly in minimizing the number of colors, and secondly, scaling the pattern to the wall — the bigger the surface the bigger the pattern should be. These are neat tricks I have used in many projects.

WE SEE REPEATED patterns in tiling, wall divider screening and bathroom floor in the hotel design on Beth's trip to Mexico with her mother. When she redecorates the house, the wallpaper also takes on a geometric abstract feel.

TWELVE

VELVET

The pink and green complementary combination
was popular in the Queen's Gambit as seen on this
green velvet sofa.

Velvet was an important and tactile fabric in the modern age. Again, like gold, it was that touch of suburban luxury the regular person craved. It is also very appropriate to dress the simple graphic modern shapes of furniture. We see sofas and armchairs upholstered in teal velvet in the Queen's Gambit but any richly-hued fabric will achieve instant visual impact.

This red seating area suits a hotel coffee bar and contrasts well with the checkerboard flooring and large indoor potted palms.

Natural materials play a big part in midcentury
modern design.

HOT TIP: use velvet in contrast. For examples, an entire wall sheeted in smooth plywood paneling forms an industrial contrast with the luxuriously soft velvet sofa.

THIRTEEN
TABLE LAMPS

Table lamps have dropped in popularity recently (since the 2000s) due to over-reliance on electronic equipment and screens, the blue light glare of which competes with the warm glow of the lamp. Lighting is very important and yet understated in midcentury modern design.

A nightstand table lamp

Lamps cast light downwards, which is flattering on the skin.

Brightening the corner where you are: large corner table lamps
provide a surprising amount of light.

HOT TIP: Big drum lampshade. Ironically they make a tight
corner appear bigger. They are a lot more attractive and efficient than

little lamps. Many scenes in the Queen's Gambit take place in moody lighting in the bedroom or living room. Lamps instantly make an intimate setting.

FOURTEEN

TEAL

TEAL IS A VERY striking classic interior color. It's a versatile blue-green or green-blue which works well not just in midcentury modern design but eclectic or traditional themes too. It can set off and balance any hard-to-match colors such as pink and of course, easy neutrals like black and white of the chessboard.

Its name is believed to have been taken from the small freshwater teal duck whose eyes are surrounded by this color. Teal is medium blue-green, and depending on the light and your eyesight, it could appear medium green or a dark cyan. It has a yellow undertone, is close to turquoise, and its most muted version is a green slate. As its use can be both loud or quiet, it suits both the vintage and the contemporary room. The jewel-blue base radiates sea calm and tranquility. The yellow undertone is fresh and uplifting.

HOT TIP: The complementary opposite of teal on the color wheel is coral, so when paired, the effect is very dramatic. As a color that was popular in the midcentury, when combined with gold tones it will still create that vintage look.

Adjacent hues on the wheel are called analogous and used together, rather than the dramatic impact, you will be able to create a relaxed feel. Analogous shades with teal are blue, green, purple and yellow.

Teal can be used as an accent on a bold and bright feature wall or it can be a muted backdrop to other features or textures. As in midcentury modern design principles, the art is in the balance.

Analogous hues used together: wall of green botanical wallpaper,
a table with hairpin legs and a velvet sofa match a teal wall to
produce a calm and deeply reflective interior.

FIFTEEN

PLAID

PLAID WALLPAPER HAS A COUNTRY HOTEL, hunting lodge or cozy getaway connotations but it is equally at home in the urban or suburban environment, as we have seen in the Queen's Gambit.

It's a very smart approach to high traffic areas, and that is why hotels favor it for both the floor and the walls. The checkered busy pattern eliminates the need for a lot of pictures or decorations and it hides scuffs and uneven surfaces well, especially in old buildings.

Broadly speaking, a busy wallpaper pattern is good for dimly lit or small spaces because you can divert the focus to internal rather than external. It is a really good trick of the eye. Plaid looks very good in settings when floral wallpaper is too feminine. Plaid is gender-neutral and non-ageist. It looks right in both a retiree's study or a children's room.

When matched with the same carpet it commands a serious "banker's home office" impact. I have used plaid in a New York basement apartment where it still looks very smart as it functions well in rooms where there is little natural daylight, and this shows the versatility of this pattern. **HOT TIP:** Avoid red or greens. You don't want Christmas all year round.

COCKTAILS

ONCE YOU HAVE your mood lighting sorted, no midcentury modern evening is complete without these class act classics. They take no more than 5 minutes each. **HOT TIP:** put some vintage music on and make these very easy and mess-free pre-dinner drinks.

GIBSON

A Gibson cocktail is similar to a martini, but instead of the olives are the pickled cocktail onions, adding umami. Alma is seen to favor the Gibson over the martini when she's on the flight with Beth to Cincinnati.

Serves 1

- 60ml (2 fl oz) gin
- 1 teaspoon dry vermouth
- Half cup ice cubes
- Cocktail stick
- 2-3 small silver skin pickled onions

1. Chill the cocktail glass in the fridge or freezer.
2. Singe the onions in a non-stick frying pan to brown them for about 4-5 minutes. Set aside and allow to cool.
3. Put the gin, vermouth and ice cubes into a mixing jug and stir for 30 seconds to dilute. Strain into a chilled cocktail glass.
4. To garnish, thread the cooled onions onto a cocktail stick.

MARGARITA

Alma Wheatley ran up a considerable account on margaritas in the Aztec Palace hotel on the Mexican tour. It's a classic tequila cocktail using triple sec and lime juice. Don't forget to serve in a salt-rimmed martini glass.

Serves 1

- 6oml 2 fl oz tequila
- 1.5 tbsp lime juice
- Wedge of lime
- 1 tbsp triple sec
- Half cup ice
- Salt
- Slice of lime to garnish

1. Chill a martini glass in the fridge or freezer.
2. Dust a little salt on a saucer. Wipe the martini glass rim with a wedge of lime. Remove the glass from the fridge or freezer and turn it upside down, imprinting in the salt, and twisting it by the stem to coat. Return glass to upright

position.

3. Shake the ice, tequila, lime juice, triple sec in a cocktail shaker. Strain into a chilled martini glass served with a slice of lime.

MARTINI

There are many versions of the martini, such as the dry, wet, dirty and perfect. This is a classic (stirred not shaken).

Serves 1

- 60ml (2 fl oz) vodka or gin
- 1 tbsp dry vermouth
- Half cup ice cubes
- Olive on a cocktail stick or lemon peel to garnish

1. Chill the martini glass in the fridge or freezer.
2. Combine the gin or vodka, dry vermouth and the ice in a mixing jug. Stir for 30 seconds to dilute.
3. Strained into a chilled martini glass. Thread the olive onto a cocktail stick and garnish. Alternatively, serve with a twist of lemon peel.

And cheers. Hope the ideas have taken you on a midcentury modern design journey. May we live a life more fabulous.

IF YOU ARE EXCITED **by the idea of entertaining at home but don't know where to start,** *Quick and Easy Party Treats: for Special Occasions* is perfect for busy beginners. Included are 5 modern healthy appetizers anyone can prepare, and my bonus ORIGINAL Asian-inspired cocktail, Halong Bay. Read *Quick and Easy Party Treats: for Special Occasions.*

Love modernism? The merch bar is open. The Architecture and Interior Design collection includes T-shirts, fridge magnets and stationery all designed by me. Hipsters and design fans will appreciate the competitively-priced, amusing and charming original art gifts. Go and have a browse in the merch bar.

BEFORE YOU GO

The book you are holding in your hand is the result of my dream to be an author. I hope you enjoyed it as much as I enjoyed writing it. I am slowly building my author brand, ranking and profile. As you've probably suspected, it takes weeks, months or years to write a book. It exists through dedication, passion and love. Reviews help persuade others to give my books a shot. More readers will motivate me to write, which means more books. I love connecting with and hearing from you. I personally read each review you write. It gives me a sense of fulfilment and meaning— you read my book, I read your review. It will take *less than a minute* and can be just a line to say what you liked or didn't. If you could do me just this one favor and help me, I would be ever so grateful. Please leave me a review on wherever you bought this book. A big thank you. *Ivy*

"The longer I live the more beautiful life becomes."
- Frank Lloyd Wright

ABOUT THE AUTHOR

I. Ngeow was born and raised in Johor Bahru, Malaysia. A multi-award-winning author, Ivy has been in the practice of architecture and interior design for more than 25 years after qualifying from the University of New South Wales in Sydney, Australia and Kingston University in the UK. An architecture and interiors columnist for Wimbledon Time and Leisure magazine for 7 years, she started her own firm in 2001.

 She specializes in high-end luxury and vintage industrial design. An international expert in her field, she has worked on residential properties in New York and London, "vacay" homes in the Hamptons, Caribbean resorts, Gleneagles Spa Resort in Scotland, Claridges Hotel in London and boutique hotels in Havana and Penang, two UNESCO World Heritage sites. Her vintage industrial experience includes low-budget, sustainable pop-up retail cubes for stationery and clothes, and a world tour equipment storage unit warehouse for a top successful band.

An author of novels and short stories, Ivy holds an MA in Writing from Middlesex University, where she won the 2005 Middlesex University Literary Press Prize out of almost 1500

entrants worldwide. Her debut *Cry of the Flying Rhino* (2017) was awarded the 2016 International Proverse Prize.

Her interests include impromptu virtuoso piano performances, health and fitness, beauty and sewing.

You can find her here:

Architecture and interior design: www.ivyngeow.com
Writing: www.writengeow.com
Twitter: (twitter.com/ivyngeow)
Facebook: (facebook.com/ivyngeowwriter)
Instagram: (www.instagram.com/ivyngeow)
Email: ivy_ngeow AT yahoo DOT com

PHOTO CREDITS

Printed in Great Britain
by Amazon